BACH

THE FIRST BOOK FOR PIANISTS

Edited by

Willard A. Palmer

Johann Sebastian Bach (1685-1750)

CONTENTS

The selections included in this book are taken from "BACH – An Introduction to his Keyboard Music." For students and teachers who prefer an expanded introductory section and additional selections in a 64 page book, the publisher recommends the Bach introduction listed above.

Most collections of easy Bach pieces contain simplified arrangements. Even the simplest selections from the *Notebook for Anna Magdalena* are usually further simplified. Ornaments are generally omitted or incorrectly notated or realized. Few editors have bothered to refer to the original manuscripts to ensure the presentation of a correct text, and even those editions known as "urtexts" are often inaccurate.

All the pieces in this book are in their original form, unsimplified. They have been thoroughly researched from the original manuscripts. In some cases, these are in J.S. Bach's own handwriting. Some are manuscripts written by members of the family or by his students. In each case, all known early sources have been carefully consulted. All of the notes and ornaments in dark print are from these original sources. The indications in light gray print are editorial suggestions based on careful study of the proper performance of Bach's music.

(continued on page 24)

The *menuet* (men-you-ET) is a dance of French origin. It is said that King Louis XIV danced the "very first" menuet, composed by Lully in 1653. Menuets were originally played at a very moderate tempo but later took on considerably more speed. They should always be played with graceful dignity.

MENUET
IN D MINOR

from the *Notebook for Anna Magdalena*

10
f
mp
13
16
f
19
mp
22

MENUET
IN B♭ MAJOR

from the Notebook for Anna Magdalena

13
16
mp
cresc.
20
mf
23
1.
2.
mp
mp

MARCH
IN D MAJOR

from the *Notebook*
for Anna Magdalena

ⓐ This ornament combines the long appoggiatura and the trill. This is also an example of "over-dotting." See the explanation under DOTTED RHYTHMS on page 24.

10
p
simile
13
16
mf
cresc.
19
f

MENUET
IN G MAJOR

from the *Notebook*
for Anna Magdalena

17
p
21
25
f
29

In the baroque period, menuets were often played in pairs. This menuet and the one on pages 8 and 9 were probably meant to be played in this way. First play the menuet on pages 8 and 9, then play this menuet, then play the first menuet again, without repeats.

MENUET
IN G MINOR

from the *Notebook for Anna Magdalena*

ⓐ The trill may have a termination: 

A musette is an instrument of the bagpipe family. Selections titled *Musette* were originally imitations of that instrument. The melody of this selection resembles those played by the bagpipe, and the basses almost have a droning effect. This style of bass writing, with repeated octaves, was called "murky bass."

MUSETTE
IN D MAJOR

from the *Notebook for Anna Magdalena*

A more accurate imitation of a musette may be achieved by playing the entire selection with a continuous legato, with the same level of dynamics throughout.

14
cresc.
17
f
20
f
23
26

MARCH
IN G MAJOR

from the *Notebook for Anna Magdalena*

Giocoso M.M. ♩ = 104 - 112

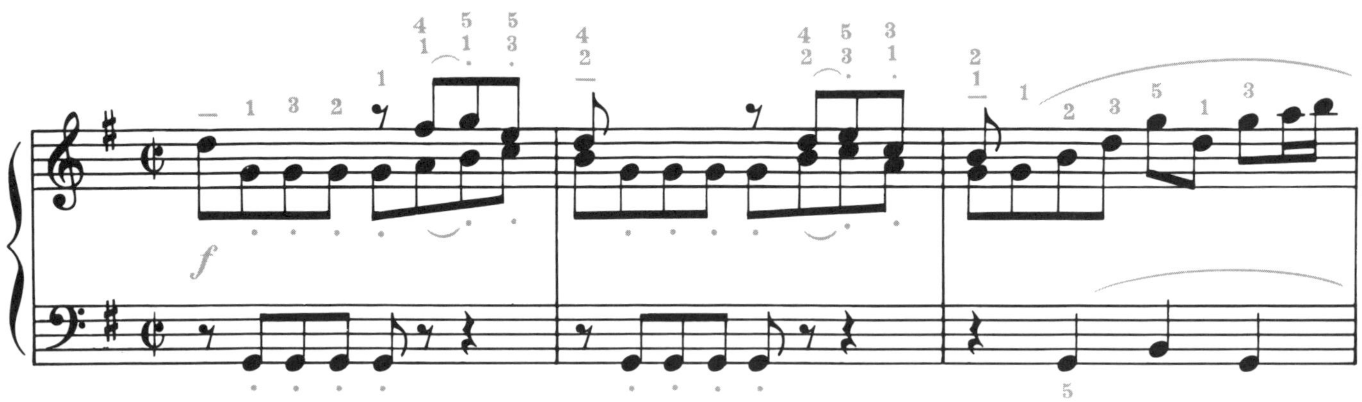

ⓐ This is an example of "over-dotting." See the explanation under DOTTED RHYTHMS on page 24.

10
mp
13
mf
16
19
tr

The *Polonaise* is one of the national dances of Poland. It is always in moderate triple meter. It is more a promenade or processional than a dance. One of its characteristic rhythms is the figure , which is found in many of the *polonaises* of Chopin.

POLONAISE

IN G MINOR

from the *Notebook for Anna Magdalena*

Allegro moderato M.M. ♩ = 92-100

(a) The dotted rhythm may be exaggerated here and in the 5th measure.

The first measure would be played:  See DOTTED RHYTHMS on page 24.

MUSETTE
FROM "ENGLISH SUITE" IN G MINOR

For a more accurate imitation of a musette, this piece may be played with continuous legato, with the same dynamic level throughout.

MENUET
IN G MINOR

from the *Little Clavier Book for W. F. Bach*

PRELUDE
IN C MAJOR

PRELUDE
IN G MINOR

from the *Little Clavier Book for W. F. Bach*

Andante moderato ♩= 96

PRELUDE
IN C MINOR

This selection is sometimes called "The Lute Prelude," because it was composed for Lute. Bach may have played it on his own Lute-Clavecin (a harpsichord fitted with Lute strings).

13
p
poco cresc.
16
poco dim.
19
22
dim
25
in
u

28
en
do
p
31
34
poco cresc
en
37
do
dim.
40
p poco rit.
mf

(continued from page 1)

ORNAMENTATION

The ornaments used in this book are the trill, appoggiatura, mordent, and schleifer. The realizations in light print above the staffs show how to play them. The basic rules for playing Bach's ornaments are summarized below:

Ornaments are written in small notes or in symbols above or below the notes.

All of Bach's ornaments begin on the beat of the main (full-sized) note and take their time value away from the main note.

- The *trill*, indicated by *tr* or 𝆖 , begins on the upper auxiliary (next higher scale tone). It must have at least four notes but may have as many as the tempo of the piece and the value of the note will allow.

  The trill may end with an anticipation of the following note, or with a termination consisting of two notes (the lower auxiliary and the main note), which are played at the same speed as the trill.

- The *appoggiaturas* (♪) which appear in this book are indicated by small eighth notes. These are long appoggiaturas. They receive half the value of the following note. (If the following note is a dotted note, the appoggiatura generally receives 2/3 the value. In some cases they sound better when given only 1/3 the value of the dotted note.) Appoggiaturas should be accented and the main note played more softly.

- The *mordent* (𝆗) is a "biting" ornament. The main note is quickly alternated with its lower auxiliary.

- The *schleifer* 𝆖 is a "sliding" ornament, usually used to fill in the gap between a note and the previous one. An example of its correct performance is shown on page 2, in the 6th measure.

DOTTED RHYTHMS

In baroque music, dotted rhythms were sometimes expected to be played in an exaggerated fashion, lengthening the value of the dotted note and shortening the following short note proportionately:

This practice was called "over-dotting." Where over-dotting is appropriate in the pieces in this book, it is shown in the light-print realizations above the staffs.

The Bach Family
Portrait by Toby Rosenthal